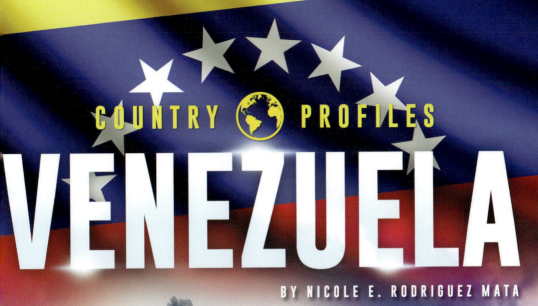

COUNTRY PROFILES
VENEZUELA

BY NICOLE E. RODRIGUEZ MATA

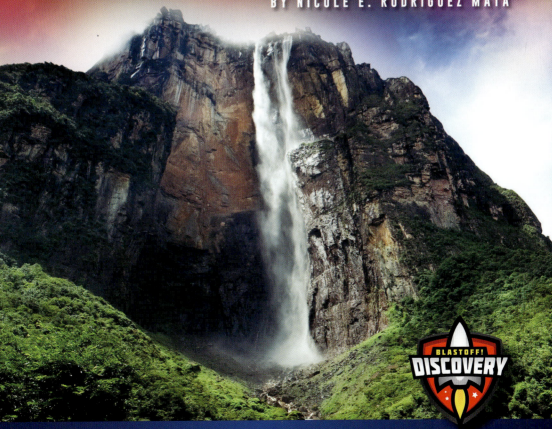

BELLWETHER MEDIA • MINNEAPOLIS, MN

This edition first published in 2023 by Bellwether Media, Inc.

No part of this publication may be reproduced in whole or in part without written permission of the publisher.
For information regarding permission, write to Bellwether Media, Inc., Attention: Permissions Department,
6012 Blue Circle Drive, Minnetonka, MN 55343.

Library of Congress Cataloging-in-Publication Data

Names: Rodriguez Mata, Nicole E., author.
Title: Venezuela / by Nicole E. Rodriguez Mata.
Description: Minneapolis, MN : Bellwether Media, Inc., 2023. | Series: Blastoff! Discovery : country profiles | Includes bibliographical references and index. | Audience: Ages 7-13 | Audience: Grades 4-6 | Summary: "Engaging images accompany information about Venezuela. The combination of high-interest subject matter and narrative text is intended for students in grades 3 through 8"– Provided by publisher.
Identifiers: LCCN 2022017359 (print) | LCCN 2022017360 (ebook) | ISBN 9781644877500 (library binding) | ISBN 9781648347962 (ebook)
Subjects: LCSH: Venezuela–Juvenile literature.
Classification: LCC F2308.5 .R64 2023 (print) | LCC F2308.5 (ebook) | DDC 987–dc23/eng/20220415
LC record available at https://lccn.loc.gov/2022017359
LC ebook record available at https://lccn.loc.gov/2022017360

Text copyright © 2023 by Bellwether Media, Inc. BLASTOFF! DISCOVERY and associated logos are trademarks and/or registered trademarks of Bellwether Media, Inc.

Editors: Rebecca Sabelko and Christina Leaf
Designer: Brittany McIntosh

Printed in the United States of America, North Mankato, MN.

TABLE OF CONTENTS

MORROCOY NATIONAL PARK	4
LOCATION	6
LANDSCAPE AND CLIMATE	8
WILDLIFE	10
PEOPLE	12
COMMUNITIES	14
CUSTOMS	16
SCHOOL AND WORK	18
PLAY	20
FOOD	22
CELEBRATIONS	24
TIMELINE	26
VENEZUELA FACTS	28
GLOSSARY	30
TO LEARN MORE	31
INDEX	32

MORROCOY NATIONAL PARK

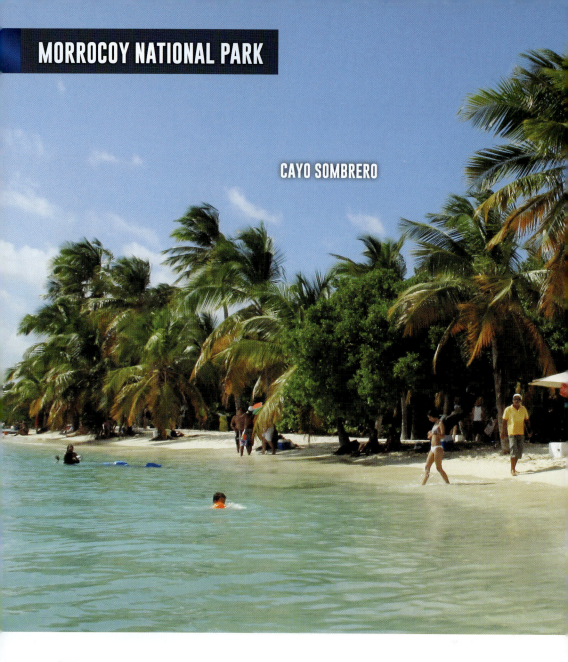

CAYO SOMBRERO

A family sits in a small boat. They are ready for the beach at Morrocoy National Park! Bags and towels sit between them. They are going to the Cayo Sombrero beach. The boat cruises past forests of **mangroves**. The trees stand high on their roots as if on stilts.

OTHER TOP SITES

KEREPAKUPAI MERÚ (ANGEL FALLS)

LOS ROQUES

MÉDANOS DE CORO NATIONAL PARK

PICO BOLÍVAR

    A small, dark gray dolphin swims next to the boat, racing the family. As they get closer to Cayo Sombrero, they spot the white sand beach in the distance. Finally, they arrive. The water is bright blue and clear. Venezuela is full of natural wonders!

LOCATION

The Bolivarian Republic of Venezuela is a country in northern South America. It covers 352,144 square miles (912,050 square kilometers). The capital, Caracas, is located in north-central Venezuela. The city sits in a high valley of a coastal mountain range.

Venezuela borders the Caribbean Sea and the Atlantic Ocean to the north. To the east is Guyana, and to the south is Brazil. Colombia lies to the west. Venezuela has many islands. The most popular include Margarita Island, Los Roques, and La Tortuga.

NATURAL PLAYGROUND

Waraira Repano National Park, also called El Ávila, protects many of the mountains surrounding Caracas. A cable car connects the park with the city. City dwellers head to the park to hike, bike, and enjoy nature.

CARIBBEAN SEA

CARACAS

VALENCIA

ATLANTIC OCEAN

BARQUISIMETO

VENEZUELA

GUYANA

BRAZIL

LANDSCAPE AND CLIMATE

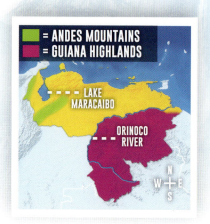

The enormous Lake Maracaibo lies in northwestern Venezuela. Lowlands surround the lake and much of the northern coast. They rise into the snow-capped peaks of the Andes Mountains. East of the Andes lie Los Llanos. The Orinoco River cuts through these **plains**. In the east and south, **plateaus** called *tepuis* rise in the Guiana Highlands. **Tropical** forests cover parts of the country.

KEREPAKUPAI MERÚ

A TALL FALLS
Kerepakupai Merú, also called Angel Falls, is the world's highest waterfall at 3,212 feet (979 meters) tall. It drops off the Auyán-Tepui plateau.

CARACAS
Average seasonal highs and lows

JANUARY
HIGH: 79 °F (26 °C)
LOW: 62 °F (17 °C)

APRIL
HIGH: 83 °F (28 °C)
LOW: 67 °F (19 °C)

JULY
HIGH: 81 °F (27 °C)
LOW: 67 °F (19 °C)

OCTOBER
HIGH: 82 °F (28 °C)
LOW: 67 °F (19 °C)

°F = degrees Fahrenheit
°C = degrees Celsius

Most of Venezuela has a tropical climate. The hot temperature changes little throughout the year. Most regions only have two seasons. From May to October, constant rain marks the wet season. Typically, the rain disappears for the dry season in December through March.

WILDLIFE

There is a huge variety of animals that live in Venezuela. Troupials are the national bird. They fly over the plains and in low mountain regions. In the Andes, spectacled bears roam the mountainsides looking for fruits. Mountain coatis wander mountain forests. They sniff out food with their long snouts.

Chigüires munch on water plants in the marshes of Los Llanos. There, bright scarlet ibises gather in large groups. They watch for hungry caimans. Amazon River dolphins swim in the Orinoco River. Macaws fill Venezuela's forests with bright colors. They like to perch in pairs.

TROUPIAL

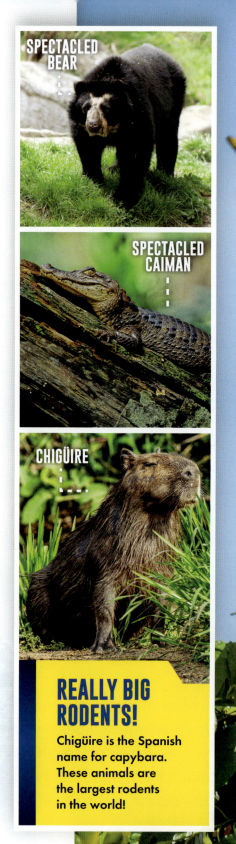

SPECTACLED BEAR

SPECTACLED CAIMAN

CHIGÜIRE

REALLY BIG RODENTS!

Chigüire is the Spanish name for capybara. These animals are the largest rodents in the world!

PEOPLE

FAR FROM HOME

Venezuelans love their country. However, political and economic issues in recent years have led more than 6 million people to leave their homeland. Some went to neighboring countries like Brazil. Others went as far as the United Arab Emirates.

There are almost 30 million Venezuelans. Most Venezuelans have a mix of African, **Indigenous**, and European **ancestors**. Around one in five people can trace their **heritage** to Spain and other European countries. Around 51 Indigenous groups make up a small number of Venezuela's population. The largest groups are the Goajiro and Warao.

Religion is very important in Venezuelan **culture**. Most Venezuelans are Roman Catholic. A small number are Protestant Christian, Jewish, or other religions. The official language is Spanish. Some people also speak Indigenous languages.

FAMOUS FACE
Name: Simón Díaz
Birthday: August 8, 1928
Died: February 19, 2014
Hometown: Barbacoas, Venezuela
Famous for: Known as Uncle Simón, he spent his life sharing Venezuelan music and folklore with the world

SPEAK SPANISH

ENGLISH	SPANISH	HOW TO SAY IT
hello	hola	OH-la
goodbye	chao	CHOW
please	por favor	pohr fah-VOR
thank you	gracias	grah-SEE-ahs
yes	sí	SEE
no	no	noh

CARACAS

COMMUNITIES

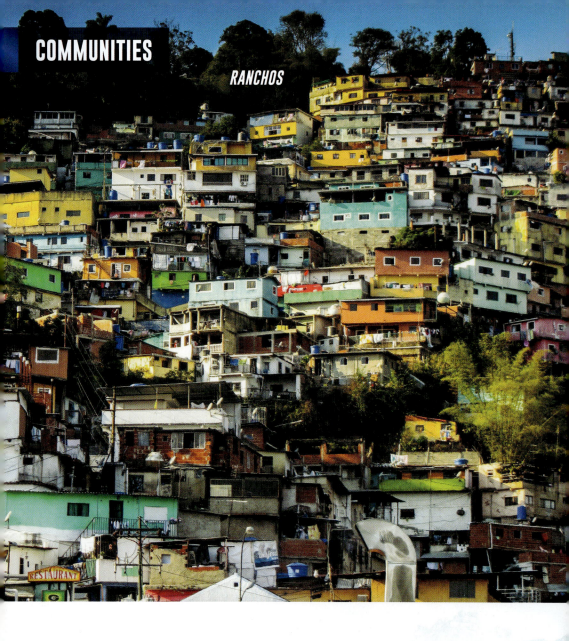

RANCHOS

Over 8 out of 10 people in Venezuela live in cities. Many Venezuelans live in houses or apartment buildings. Others live in colorful shacks called *ranchos* on the outskirts of large cities like Caracas. It is common for families to live with multiple generations in one home. **Urban** Venezuelans usually use public transportation and motorcycles to avoid city traffic.

Rural towns are small. Poorly maintained roads and a lack of public transportation make it hard to get around. In many rural towns, water, electricity, and food are hard to find. Still, the people in the community stand together and help each other out.

LIFE ON THE WATER
Palafitos are found by Lake Maracaibo. These houses are built over water on stilts!

PALAFITO

CUSTOMS

Venezuelans are outgoing people. They speak loudly and express themselves with their hands. To say hello, women greet others with a kiss on each cheek. Men typically shake hands. Everyone shares hugs with close family and friends. Venezuelans often use touch to express affection.

A FAVORITE SONG
The joropo song "Alma Llanera" is the unofficial national anthem of Venezuela.

Music and art are very important in Venezuela. Joropo is a **traditional** type of music and dance from Los Llanos. It uses the Venezuelan cuatro, a small four-string guitar. Salsa and merengue are other popular musical styles. Modern painting and sculpture art are very popular in Venezuela.

SCHOOL AND WORK

Children in Venezuela receive nine years of basic education. Classes are taught in Spanish. Students study in one of two educational paths for their last two years. One path focuses on sciences, while the other focuses on arts and **humanities**. Education is free at all levels, although it is also common for children to go to private schools.

Many Venezuelans have **service jobs**. The nation's many cultural sites and natural wonders offer jobs in **tourism**. Venezuela's huge **oil reserves** create many jobs. People work to remove, **refine**, and **export** oil. Farms produce tropical crops like coffee, bananas, and sugarcane.

FARMING COFFEE

OIL WORKERS

PLAY

BASEBALL

The most popular sport in Venezuela is baseball. Many Venezuelan players, such as José Altuve, end up playing on North American Major League Baseball teams. Soccer is also popular. Fans across the nation cheer on the national team, La Vinotinto. Adults and children play on club teams or in their neighborhoods.

SOCCER

Venezuelans love going to the beach. They bring coolers full of food and spend all day enjoying the sun and clear water. People also explore mountains by hiking or taking the cable car in Mérida or Caracas. Playing videos games is another activity that many Venezuelans enjoy.

BEACH

MARACAS

Maracas are an instrument with a long history in Venezuela. They are common in joropo songs. You can make your own maracas to shake!

What You Need:
- paper plate
- stapler and staples
- dry beans
- markers

What You Do:
1. Fold the paper plate in half.
2. Staple around the round edge. Leave a gap of about 3 inches (8 centimeters) near the top.
3. Drop a handful of beans into the gap.
4. Finish stapling the last 3 inches.
5. Decorate with yellow, blue, and red to match the Venezuelan flag!

FOOD

MAKING AREPAS

For breakfast, many Venezuelans eat corn cakes called *arepas*. Fried cheese sticks called *tequeños* and bread rolls stuffed with ham called *cachitos* are also popular. With their breakfast, children usually have a dark, fizzy malt drink called Malta. Adults often drink coffee with their breakfast.

Lunch is the largest meal of the day. *Pabellón criollo* is the national dish of Venezuela. It consists of black beans, shredded beef, white rice, and fried plantains. Dinner is often light. It can include arepas or *empanadas*. Simple versions only have cheese, but people can stuff them with whatever they like.

TEQUEÑOS
PABELLÓN CRIOLLO

CHICHA

Have an adult help you make this sweet, creamy drink!

Ingredients:
2 cups of white rice
4 cups of water
1 can of sweetened condensed milk
ground cinnamon

Steps:
1. Cook the rice in the water until it is very soft. There should still be some water left over in the pot when the rice is cooked.
2. Pour the rice and water into a blender. Add the sweetened condensed milk.
3. Blend until it is smooth.
4. Serve in a glass with ice and top with a sprinkle of cinnamon.

CELEBRATIONS

Venezuelans celebrate the New Year with family, friends, and dancing! Many people pack a suitcase and walk around their neighborhood. This is believed to bring travel throughout the year. People also eat 12 grapes just before midnight. They make a wish for each grape eaten.

The Corpus Christi festival takes place each June. Masked devils dance and play maracas in the streets. Each Christmas, families make *pan de jamón*, or ham bread, and *hallacas*, which include cornmeal dough stuffed with meat and cooked in banana leaves. Families may trade hallacas as a sign of friendship. They show love for each other and their culture!

CHRISTMAS PAN DE JAMÓN

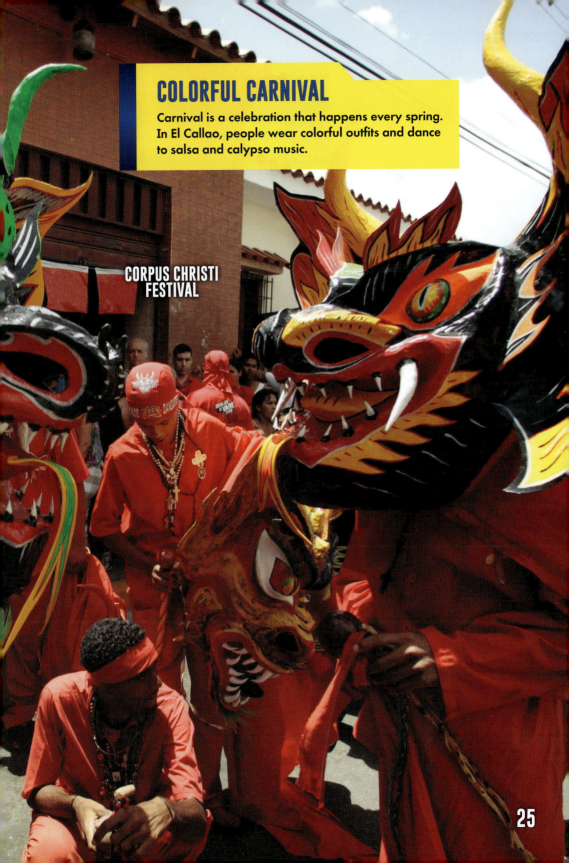

COLORFUL CARNIVAL

Carnival is a celebration that happens every spring. In El Callao, people wear colorful outfits and dance to salsa and calypso music.

CORPUS CHRISTI FESTIVAL

TIMELINE

1521
The Spanish begin to colonize what is now Venezuela

AROUND 100 BCE TO 1500 CE
Many Indigenous peoples thrive in what is now Venezuela, such as the Timoto-Cuica who farmed in the Andes

1811
Venezuela declares independence from Spain

1498
Christopher Columbus and Alonso de Ojeda visit the area for the first time

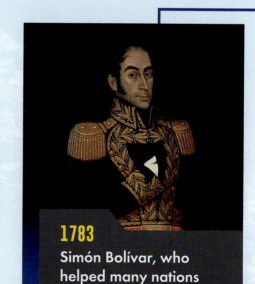

1783
Simón Bolívar, who helped many nations in South America gain independence from Spain, is born in Caracas

1908–1935
Venezuela becomes the world's largest oil exporter

2021
Yulimar Rojas sets the world record for Women's Triple Jump and wins an Olympic gold medal

1958
The Venezuelan navy and air force drive the harsh dictator Marcos Pérez Jiménez out of power

1830
Venezuela leaves Gran Colombia, a republic formed in 1819 that included what is now Venezuela, Colombia, Panama, and Ecuador

1998
Hugo Chavez is elected president

VENEZUELA FACTS

Official Name: Bolivarian Republic of Venezuela

Flag of Venezuela: Venezuela's flag has three bands of color. Yellow is at the top. It symbolizes the riches of the land. Blue represents the waters of the Caribbean Sea. Red stands for the blood shed for independence. The eight stars in the middle of the blue band represent the original eight provinces. Government flags include the national coat of arms in the top left corner.

Area: 352,144 square miles (912,050 square kilometers)

Capital City: Caracas

Important Cities: Maracaibo, Valencia, Barquisimeto, Maracay

Population: 29,789,730 (2022 est.)

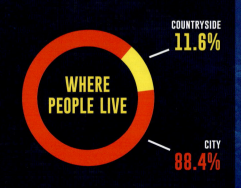

WHERE PEOPLE LIVE
COUNTRYSIDE 11.6%
CITY 88.4%

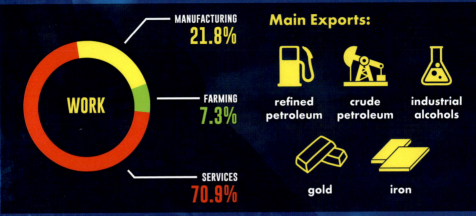

Main Exports:
refined petroleum, crude petroleum, industrial alcohols, gold, iron

WORK: MANUFACTURING 21.8%, FARMING 7.3%, SERVICES 70.9%

National Holiday:
Independence Day, July 5

Main Language:
Spanish (official)

Form of Government:
federal presidential republic

Title for Country Leader:
president

RELIGION: PROTESTANT 2%, OTHER 2%, ROMAN CATHOLIC 96%

Unit of Money:
Bolívar

29

GLOSSARY

ancestors—relatives who lived long ago

culture—the beliefs, arts, and ways of life in a place or society

export—to sell to another country

heritage—the traditions, achievements, and beliefs that are part of the history of a group of people

humanities—branches of learning that study human-made areas, such as languages, literature, and art

indigenous—related to a group of people that began in the area

mangroves—tropical trees that can grow along coasts in salty swamp water

oil reserves—amounts of oil that can be taken out of the earth

plains—large areas of flat land

plateaus—areas of flat, raised land

refine—to clean or process a substance or make it free of unwanted material

rural—related to the countryside

service jobs—jobs that perform tasks for people or businesses

tourism—the business of people traveling to visit other places

traditional—related to customs, ideas, or beliefs handed down from one generation to the next

tropical—related to the tropics; the tropics is a hot, rainy region near the equator.

urban—related to cities and city life

TO LEARN MORE

AT THE LIBRARY

Anderson, Corey. *Hola, Venezuela*. Ann Arbor, Mich.: Cherry Lake Publishing, 2020.

Engle, Margarita. *Dancing Hands: How Teresa Carreño Played the Piano for President Lincoln*. New York, N.Y.: Atheneum Books for Young Readers, 2019.

Tustison, Matt. *José Altuve: Baseball Star*. Lake Elmo, Minn.: Focus Readers, 2019.

ON THE WEB

Factsurfer.com gives you a safe, fun way to find more information.

1. Go to www.factsurfer.com.

2. Enter "Venezuela" into the search box and click 🔍.

3. Select your book cover to see a list of related content.

INDEX

activities, 4, 7, 21
Altuve, José, 20
Andes Mountains, 8, 10
Angel Falls (see Kerepakupai
    Merú)
art, 17, 18
capital (see Caracas)
Caracas, 6, 7, 9, 13, 14, 21
Carnival, 25
celebrations, 24–25
Christmas, 24
climate, 9
communities, 14–15
Corpus Christi, 24, 25
customs, 16–17
Díaz, Simón, 13
education, 18
fast facts, 28–29
food, 22–23, 24
housing, 14, 15
islands, 6
Kerepakupai Merú, 9
Lake Maracaibo, 8, 15
landmarks, 4, 5, 7
landscape, 4, 5, 6, 7, 8–9,
    10, 15, 21

language, 10, 13, 18
location, 6–7
Los Llanos, 8, 10, 17
maracas (activity), 21
Morrocoy National Park, 4–5
music, 17, 24, 25
New Year, 24
Orinoco River, 8, 10
people, 12–13
recipe, 23
religion, 13
size, 6
sports, 20
timeline, 26–27
transportation, 14, 15
Waraira Repano National
    Park, 7
wildlife, 5, 10–11
work, 19

The images in this book are reproduced through the courtesy of: FabioFilzi, front cover; Sergi Reboredo/ Alamy, pp. 4-5; Vadim Petrakov, pp. 5 (Kerepakupai Merú), 9 (top); ByDroneVideos, p. 5 (Los Roques); Seventov, p. 5 (Médanos de Coro National Park); Andry Rodriguez, p. 5 (Pico Bolívar); Paolo Costa, p. 8; marshalgonz, p. 9 (bottom); Natalia Kuzmina, p. 10 (troupial); Andrei Peda, p. 10 (bear); Roberto Dani, p. 10 (caiman); Gudkov Andrey, p. 10 (chigüire); Vinicius R. Souza, pp. 10-11; blickwinkel/ Alamy, p. 12; Jack Vartoogian/ Getty Image/ Contributor, p. 13 (top); Edgloris Marys, p. 13 (bottom); Ekaterina McClaud, p. 14; Prisma by Dukas Presseagentur GmbH/ Alamy, p. 15; Blend Images - Gabriela Medina/ Getty Images, p. 16; Jimmy Villalta/ VWPics/ Alamy, p. 17; Ariana Cubillos/ AP Images, p. 18; Rob Crandall/ Alamy, p. 19 (top); Jose Bula/ Alamy, p. 19 (bottom); Federico Parra/ Contributor/ Getty, p. 20 (top); muzsy, p. 20 (bottom); Eagleflying, p. 21 (top); Christina Leaf, p. 21 (bottom); Thierry Monasse/ Contributor/ Getty Images, p. 22; nehophoto, p. 23 (top); bonchan, p. 23 (middle); rjankovsky, p. 23 (bottom); acongar, p. 24; Fernando Llano/ AP Images, pp. 24-25; José Gil de Castro/ Wikipedia, p. 26; Allstar Picture Library Ltd/ Alamy, p. 27; Yuri Cortez/ Contributor/ Getty, p. 29.